Jazz Flute Etudes

Advanced Studies in Improvisation

By Marc Adler

ISBN 978-0-7935-8517-5

Houston
PUBLISHING, INC.

EXCLUSIVELY DISTRIBUTED BY

HAL•LEONARD®
CORPORATION
7777 W. BLUEMOUND RD. P.O. BOX 13819 MILWAUKEE, WI 53213

Visit Hal Leonard Online at
www.halleonard.com

INTRODUCTION

These etudes were written as my contribution to the ever expanding repertoire of etudes for the flute. As a jazz flutist I noticed, however, that there did not exist very many etudes that were written in the jazz idiom. Therefore, I decided to begin a series of etudes that would employ the "langauge" of both jazz and classical music. My wish for you is that these etudes will expand your own "vocabulary" and technique while providing a pleasurable diversion from your other etude work.

ENJOY

The enclosed etudes by Marc Adler will delight both classical and jazz musicians. Marc is an accomplished flutist and composer in both the jazz and classical arenas and is also an experienced educator. These twelve etudes explore each of the twelve keys but at the same time step out into contemporary sounds characteristic of modern jazz and 20th-century classical music, such as whole tone and diminished scales, and colorful chord progressions. Jazz flutists will enjoy his original jazz licks and may want to add some of them to their vocabulary of patterns. Classical flutists will appreciate the challenge of sight-reading these tightly woven compositions while savoring their improvisatory character.

Cynthia Folio, Ph.D.
Associate Professor
Temple University

Etude # 1

Marc Adler

This page left intentionally blank.

Etude # 2

Marc Adler

Etude # 3

Marc Adler

Etude # 3

This page left intentionally blank.

Etude # 4

Marc Adler

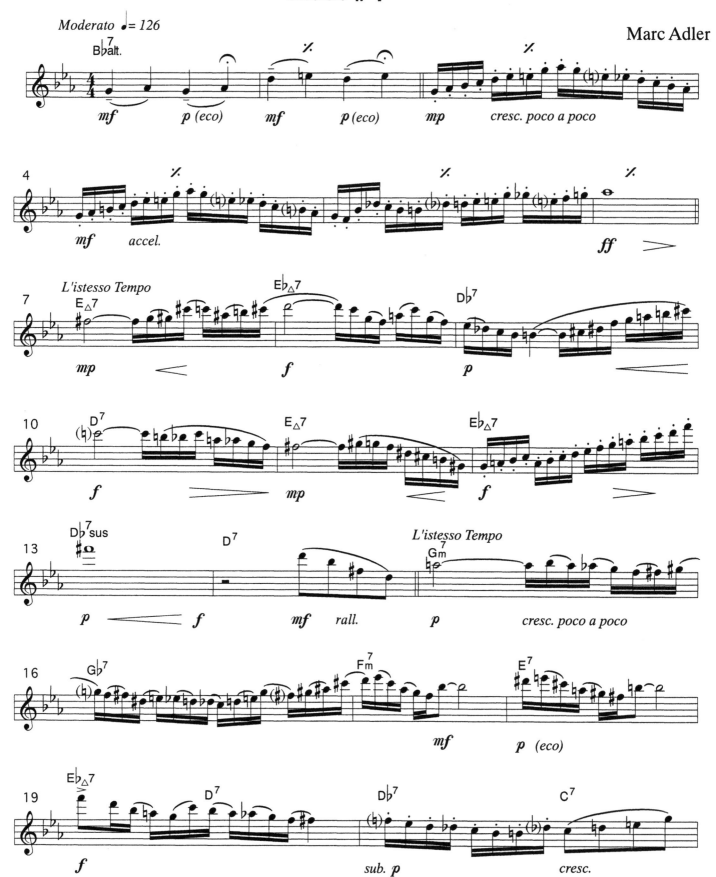

Etude # 5

Marc Adler

Etude # 6

Marc Adler

Etude # 7

Marc Adler

Etude # 8

Marc Adler

Etude # 9

Marc Adler

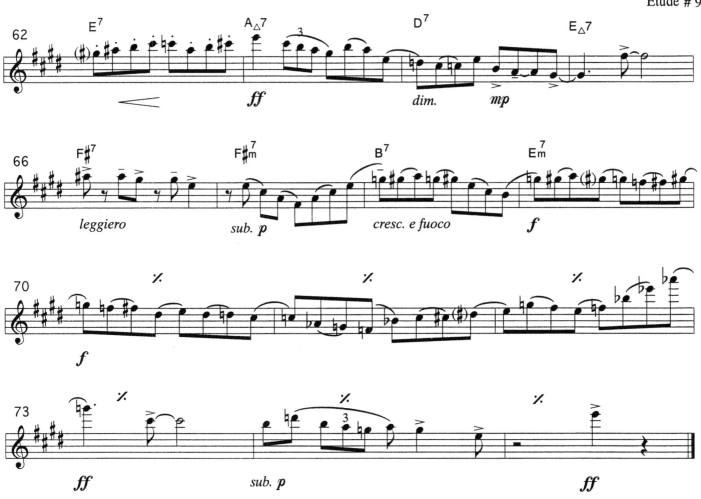

This page left intentionally blank.

Etude # 10

Marc Adler

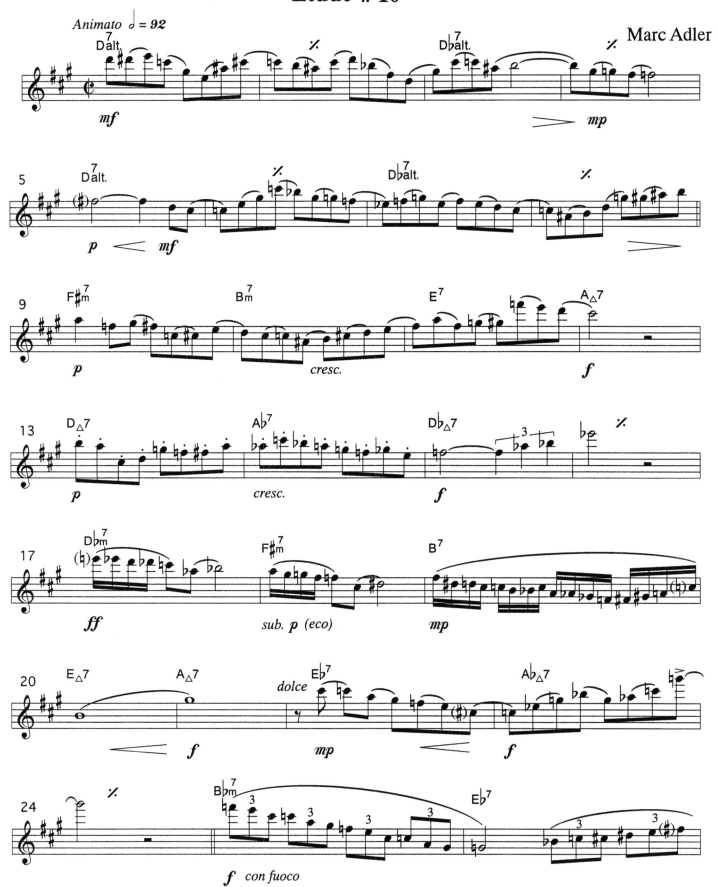

Etude # 11

Marc Adler

This page left intentionally blank.

Etude # 12

Marc Adler

Etude #13

Marc Adler

Etude #14

Marc Adler

Etude #15

Marc Adler

This page left intentionally blank.

Etude #16

Marc Adler

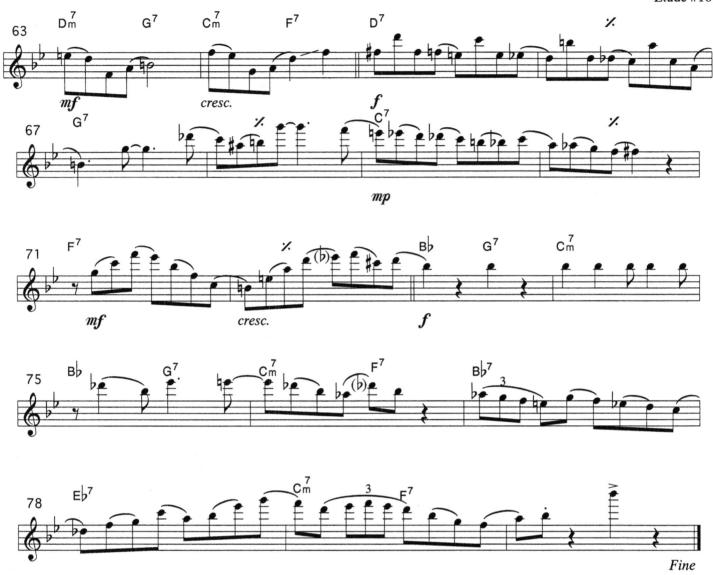

Fine